-FLORIST GUIDE-

FLOWER IDENTIFICATION

(WITH PICTURES)

ALEXIS CHRISTINE

DEDICATED TO

Gene McGonagle, my very first boss
at Ambler Flower Shop, who gave me
a chance at becoming a florist.

Table of Contents

Introduction

"What's the name of that flower?" I asked every time I was introduced to a new flower. As a beginner florist just starting out, I had no idea which flowers were which, let alone what they pair well with and how long they last. When I first started out in 2014, the world of flowers was completely new to me and I was soaking in all the knowledge I could. Now, I am sharing my knowledge with you! By the end of this book you will be able to successfully identify over 150+ flowers and you will know the properties of each flower such as how to properly pronounce their names, their durability, fragrancy, and what pairs well with each flower you are researching. This florist guide/flower identification book is perfect for florists just starting out or experienced designers wanting to learn more flowers. Thank you for interest in my guide! I hope you find it informative and helpful!

KEEP YOUR FLOWERS LOOKING FRESHER FOR LONGER!

- **KEEP FLOWERS COOL** - Keep fresh flowers away from drafts and extreme temperatures, both cold and hot, which can quickly dry out the flowers and cause wilting. Temperatures between 40-60 degrees Fahrenheit are ideal for flowers.

- **CHANGE THE WATER DAILY** - Change the water in your vase/buckets every day to boost the longevity of your flower arrangement. Clean the vase thoroughly with soapy water to remove any bacteria and be sure to rinse thoroughly.

- **ADD FLOWER FOOD** - Mix in the flower preservative according to the instructions on the packet. This will help keep the water clean.

- **FRESH CUT** - Cut the stems with a sharp knife at a 30 degree angle, about one to two inches from the bottom. This allows the stems to better absorb water. *Do not use scissors* to cut your flowers because they can crush the stems and prevent water absorption.

- **REMOVE DEAD LEAVES** or wilting leaves and debris from fresh flower arrangements to prevent it from dying prematurely.

Everyday flowers

ALSTROMERIERA

pronounced al·strow·meh·ree·uh

Colors: White, red, orange, yellow, purple, magenta, green, pink, multi color

Shelf life: 5-7 days
Season of growth: Spring-fall

Easy to pair with	★★★☆☆
Fragrancy	★★☆☆☆
Thorny	★☆☆☆☆
Durability	★★★☆☆

Pairs well with: roses, hydrangea,
gerbera daisies, salal, Italian ruscus

BUTTON MUMS

pronounced buh·tn muhmz

Colors: White, red, yellow, orange, burgundy, purple, green

Shelf life: 3-5 days
Season of growth: Summer-fall

Easy to pair with

Fragrancy

Thorny

Durability

Pairs well with: sunflowers, roses,
carnations, baker fern, salal

CARNATION

pronounced kaar·nei·shn

Colors: White, red, orange, yellow, purple, magenta, green, pink, multi color

Shelf life: 5-7 days
Season of growth: Spring-fall

Easy to pair with	★★★☆☆
Fragrancy	★☆☆☆☆
Thorny	★☆☆☆☆
Durability	★★★★☆

Pairs well with: roses, hydrangea, alstroemeria, eucalyptus, Italian ruscus

CHRYSANTHUMS

pronounced kruh·san·thuh·muhm

Colors: White, yellow, red, orange, magenta, purple, green, tan, pink

Shelf life: 3-5 days
Season of growth: Spring-summer

Easy to pair with ★★★☆☆

Fragrancy ★☆☆☆☆

Thorny ★☆☆☆☆

Durability ★★☆☆☆

Pairs well with: dahlias, roses,
carnations, baker fern, salal

DAISY

pronounced day·zee

Colors: White, yellow, orange, burgundy, purple

Shelf life: 3-5 days

Season of growth: summer-fall

Easy to pair with	★★★☆☆
Fragrancy	★☆☆☆☆
Thorny	★☆☆☆☆
Durability	★★★☆☆

Pairs well with: sunflowers, roses,
carnations, baker fern, salal

GERBERA DAISY

pronounced gur·br·uh day·zee

Colors: White, yellow, orange, red, magenta, purple, pink

Shelf life: 3-5 days
Season of growth: spring-fall

Easy to pair with	★★★☆☆
Fragrancy	★☆☆☆☆
Thorny	★☆☆☆☆
Durability	★★☆☆☆

Pairs well with: lisanthius, hypericum berries,
alstromeria, salal, Italian ruscus

HYDRANGEA

pronounced hai·dran·juh

Colors: White, blue, magenta, purple, green, pink

Shelf life: 3-5 days
Season of growth: Spring-fall

Easy to pair with

Fragrancy

Thorny

Durability

Pairs well with: Roses, ranunculus,
sunflowers, eucalyptus, Italian ruscus

IRIS

pronounced ai·ruhs

Colors: White, dark blue, light blue, yellow
Shelf life: 3-5 days
Season of growth: Summer-fall

Easy to pair with

Fragrancy

Thorny

Durability

Pairs well with: sunflowers, roses,
delphinium, eucalyptus, salal

LILY

pronounced li·lee

Colors: White, yellow, orange, burgundy, pink

Shelf life: 3-5 days
Season of growth: Year round

Easy to pair with ★★★☆☆

Fragrancy ★★★☆☆

Thorny ★☆☆☆☆

Durability ★★☆☆☆

Pairs well with: sunflowers, roses,
carnations, ruscus, salal

PEONY

pronounced pee·uh·nee

Colors: White, coral, magenta, purple, pink

Shelf life: 3-5 days

Season of growth: Summer

Easy to pair with   ★★★☆☆

Fragrancy   ★★★★☆

Thorny   ★☆☆☆☆

Durability   ★★☆☆☆

Pairs well with: lisianthus, roses,
carnations, salal, Italian ruscus

ROSE

pronounced rowz

Colors: White, yellow, red, purple, green, pink, orange, multicolor

Shelf life: 3-5 days
Season of growth: Year round

Easy to pair with	★★★★☆
Fragrancy	★★★★☆
Thorny	★★★☆☆
Durability	★★★☆☆

Pairs well with: hydrangea, ranunculus,
sunflowers, dusty Miller, Italian ruscus

SUNFLOWER

pronounced suhn·flau·ur

Colors: White, yellow, maroon, purple, multi

Shelf life: 3-5 days
Season of growth: Spring-fall

Easy to pair with

Fragrancy

Thorny

Durability

Pairs well with: roses, hypericum berries,
alstromeria eucalyptus, Italian ruscus

TEA "SPRAY" ROSE

pronounced tee.rowz

Colors: White, red, orange, yellow, purple, magenta, green, pink, multi color

Shelf life: 3-5 days
Season of growth: Spring-fall

Easy to pair with	★★★☆☆
Fragrancy	★★☆☆☆
Thorny	★★★☆☆
Durability	★★★☆☆

Pairs well with: sunflowers, hydrangea,
daisies, salal, eucalyptus

TULIP

pronounced too·luhp

Colors: White, red, orange, yellow, purple, magenta, green, pink

Shelf life: 3-5 days
Season of growth: Year round

Easy to pair with	★★★☆☆
Fragrancy	★☆☆☆☆
Thorny	★☆☆☆☆
Durability	★★★☆☆

Pairs well with: roses, hydrangea,
carnations, eucalyptus, Italian ruscus

ZINNIA

pronounced zi·nee·uh

Colors: White yellow, orange, red, magenta, purple, green, pink

Shelf life: 3-5 days
Season of growth: Summer-fall

Easy to pair with ★★★☆☆

Fragrancy ★☆☆☆☆

Thorny ★☆☆☆☆

Durability ★★☆☆☆

Pairs well with: Lisianthus, roses, carnations, salal, Italian ruscus

Line flowers

BELLS OF IRELAND

pronounced belz uhv ai·ur·luhnd

Colors: Green

Shelf life: 5-7 days

Season of growth: Spring

Easy to pair with	
Fragrancy	
Thorny	
Durability	

Pairs well with: lilies, anthurium,
gerbera daisies, baker fern, salal

DELPHINIUM

pronounced del·fi·nee·uhm

Colors: White, dark blue, light blue, purple

Shelf life: 3-5 days

Season of growth: Spring

Easy to pair with

Fragrancy

Thorny

Durability

Pairs well with: anemones, roses, carnations, baker fern, salal

GLADIOLOUS

pronounced gla·dee·ow·luhs

Colors: White, yellow, orange, red, magenta, purple, green, pink, multi

Shelf life: 5-7 days

Season of growth: Spring-summer

Easy to pair with ★★☆☆☆

Fragrancy ★★☆☆☆

Thorny ★☆☆☆☆

Durability ★★☆☆☆

Pairs well with: sunflowers, roses,
carnations, baker fern, salal

LARKSPUR

pronounced laark·spr

Colors: White, magenta, purple, pink

Shelf life: 3-5 days

Season of growth: Spring- summer

Easy to pair with

Fragrancy

Thorny

Durability

Pairs well with: gerbera daisies, roses, carnations, baker fern, salal

LIATRIS "BLAZING STAR"

pronounced lai·a·truhs

Colors: Purple, white

Shelf life: 5-7 days

Season of growth: Spring

Easy to pair with

Fragrancy

Thorny

Durability

Pairs well with: lilies, roses,
carnations, baker fern, salal

SNAP DRAGONS

pronounced snap·dra·gnz

Colors: White, yellow, red, orange, purple, pink, multi color

Shelf life: 3-5 days

Season of growth: Summer-fall

Easy to pair with

Fragrancy ★☆☆☆☆

Thorny

Durability

Pairs well with: roses, gerbera daisies,
carnations, eucalyptus, salal

Filler and Accent flowers

ASTRANTIA

pronounced uh·stran·tee·uh

Colors: White, purple, pink

Shelf life: 3-5 days
Season of growth: Spring-summer

Easy to pair with

Fragrancy

Thorny

Durability

Pairs well with: peonies, roses,
lisianthus, Italian ruscus, eucalyptus

ALLIUM BULLET

pronounced a·lee·uhm bul-it

Colors: Purple/green

Shelf life: 5-7 days

Season of growth: Summer

Easy to pair with

Fragrancy

Thorny

Durability

Pairs well with: zinnias, sunflowers,
Italian ruscus, eucalyptus

CORNFLOWER

pronounced korn·flau·ur

Colors: White, blue, purple, pink

Shelf life: 3-5 days

Season of growth: Spring-summer

Easy to pair with ★★★☆☆

Fragrancy ★★☆☆☆

Thorny ★☆☆☆☆

Durability ★☆☆☆☆

Pairs well with: hydrangea, roses, anemones, Italian ruscus, eucalyptus

COSMOS

pronounced koz·mohs

Colors: White, burgundy, hot pink, light pink

Shelf life: 3-5 days

Season of growth: Summer-fall

Easy to pair with	★★★☆☆
Fragrancy	★★☆☆☆
Thorny	★☆☆☆☆
Durability	★★☆☆☆

Pairs well with: ranunculus, roses,
peonies, Italian ruscus, salal

CRASPEDIA "BILLY BALLS"

pronounced kruh·spee·dee·uh

Colors: Yellow

Shelf life: 10-14 days
Season of growth: Spring-Fall

Easy to pair with

Fragrancy

Thorny

Durability

Pairs well with: ranunculus, roses,
gerbera daisies, Italian ruscus, salal

DIANTHUS

pronounced dai·an·thuhs

Colors: White, magenta, purple, green, pink, yellow, orange, red, multi color

Shelf life: 3-5 days
Season of growth: Spring-summer

Easy to pair with ★★★☆☆

Fragrancy ★★☆☆☆

Thorny ★☆☆☆☆

Durability ★★★☆☆

Pairs well with: hydrangea, roses,
peonies, baker fern, salal

ECHINOPS

pronounced eyk•in•aps

Colors: White, blue

Shelf life: 7-10 days
Season of growth: Summer

Easy to pair with

Fragrancy

Thorny

Durability

Pairs well with: anemone, roses,
eucalyptus, salal

GYPSOPHILA "BABIES BREATH"

pronounced gyp·soph·eel·leah

Colors: White, light yellow, light pink

Shelf life: 3-5 days
Season of growth: Spring-Fall

Easy to pair with ★★☆☆☆

Fragrancy ★☆☆☆☆

Thorny ★☆☆☆☆

Durability ★★☆☆☆

Pairs well with: lilies, roses,
ranunculus, baker fern, salal

HYPERICUM BERRIES

pronounced hai·peh·ruh·km beh·reez

Colors; Cream, red, orange, peach, green, pink

Shelf life, 5-7 days
Season of growth: Summer-Fall

Easy to pair with ★★★☆☆

Fragrancy ★☆☆☆☆

Thorny ★☆☆☆☆

Durability ★★★☆☆

Pairs well with: ranunculus, roses,
peonies , baker fern, salal

HELIPTERUM (PAPER DAISY)

pronounced hel·ip·ter·um

Colors; White, pink, hot pink

Shelf life, 3-5 days
Season of growth: Spring-fall

Easy to pair with

Fragrancy

Thorny

Durability

Pairs well with: lisianthus, roses,
carnations, eucalyptus, salal

LIMONIUM

pronounced lai·mow·nee·uhm

Colors: White, pink, yellow, purple, blue

Shelf life: 3-5 days
Season of growth: Spring-fall

Easy to pair with ★★☆☆☆

Fragrancy ★★★★☆

Thorny ★☆☆☆☆

Durability ★★☆☆☆

Pairs well with: lilies, roses,
ranunculus, baker fern, salal

MATSUMOTO ASTER

pronounced maat·soo·mow·tow a·str

Colors:Purple, pink, red, white, apricot

Shelf life: 3-5 days

Season of growth: Summer

Easy to pair with

Fragrancy

Thorny

Durability

Pairs well with: Zinnias, roses, sunflowers,
baker fern, salal

MONTE CASINO

pronounced mon·tee ca·see no

Colors: White, purple

Shelf life: 3-5 days

Season of growth: Spring-fall

Easy to pair with

Fragrancy

Thorny

Durability

Pairs well with: lilies, roses, sunflowers,
baker fern, salal

MINI CARNATIONS

pronounced mi·nee kaar·nay·shnz

Colors: White, magenta, purple, green, pink,
yellow, peach, orange, red, multi color

Shelf life: 3-5 days
Season of growth: Spring-fall

Easy to pair with ★★★☆☆

Fragrancy ★☆☆☆☆

Thorny ★☆☆☆☆

Durability ★★★☆☆

Pairs well with: Hydrangea, roses,
peonies, baker fern, salal

PEPPERCORN

pronounced peh·pr·korn

Colors: Green, pink

Shelf life: 3-5 days
Season of growth: Spring-fall

Easy to pair with	
Fragrancy	
Thorny	
Durability	

Pairs well with: hydrangea, roses,
peonies, italian ruscus, salal

PRIVET BERRIES

pronounced pri·vuht beh·ree

Colors: Green, blue

Shelf life: 3-5 days
Season of growth: Fall-winter

Easy to pair with

Fragrancy

Thorny

Durability

Pairs well with: hydrangea, roses,
anenome, eucalyptus, Italian ruscus

QUEEN ANN'S LACE

pronounced kween anz lays

Colors; White, yellow, pink, burgundy

Shelf life; 3-5 days
Season of growth: Summer-fall

Easy to pair with

Fragrancy

Thorny

Durability

Pairs well with: hydrangea, roses, peonies, eucalyptus, Italian ruscus

RICE FLOUR

pronounced rise flau·ur

Colors: White, pink

Shelf life: 3-5 days

Season of growth: Spring-fall

Easy to pair with

Fragrancy

Thorny

Durability

Pairs well with: lisanthius, roses,
peonies, eucalyptus, salal

SOLIDAGO

pronounced sow·luh·daa·gow

Colors: Yellow

Shelf life: 3-5 days
Season of growth: Summer-fall

Easy to pair with

Fragrancy

Thorny

Durability

Pairs well with: lisanthius, lilies,
gerbera daisies, baker fern, salal

STATICE

pronounced sta·tuh·s

Colors: Dark purple, light purple, pink, yellow, white

Shelf life: 5-7 days
Season of growth: Summer-fall

Easy to pair with ★★★★☆

Fragrancy ★☆☆☆☆

Thorny ★☆☆☆☆

Durability ★★★★☆

Pairs well with: ranunculus, roses,
daisies, baker fern, salal

THISTLE

pronounced thi·sl

Colors: Blue, yellow, green, white

Shelf life: 7-10 days
Season of growth: Spring-fall

Easy to pair with ★★☆☆☆

Fragrancy ★☆☆☆☆

Thorny ★★★☆☆

Durability ★★★★☆

Pairs well with: hydrangea, roses,
peonies, eucalyptus, Italian ruscus

TRICK DIANTHUS

pronounced trik dai·an·thuhs

Colors: Green

Shelf life: 7-10 days
Season of growth: Spring-fall

Easy to pair with ★★☆☆☆

Fragrancy ★☆☆☆☆

Thorny ★☆☆☆☆

Durability ★★★☆☆

Pairs well with: carnations, daisies,
zinnias, Italian ruscus, salal

TRACHELIUM

pronounced trah·kee·lee·uhm

Colors: Purple, white

Shelf life: 7-10 days
Season of growth: Summer

Easy to pair with

Fragrancy

Thorny

Durability

Pairs well with: carnations, daisies,
zinnias, Italian ruscus, salal

WAX FLOWER

pronounced waks flau·ur

Colors: White, light pink, magenta, light purple, dark purple, multi color

Shelf life: 3-5 days
Season of growth: Spring-Fall

Easy to pair with	★★★☆☆
Fragrancy	★★★★☆
Thorny	★☆☆☆☆
Durability	★★☆☆☆

Pairs well with: peonies, roses,
ranunculus, baker fern, salal

YARROW "ACHILLEA MILLEFOLIUM"

pronounced yaa·row

Colors: Yellow, burgundy, white, pink, purple

Shelf life: 3-5 days
Season of growth: Summer-fall

Easy to pair with ★★★☆☆

Fragrancy ★★☆☆☆

Thorny ★☆☆☆☆

Durability ★★★☆☆

Pairs well with: ranunculus, roses,
gerbera daisies, Italian ruscus, salal

Premium
Flowers

ALLIUM

pronounced a·lee·uhm

Colors: White, yellow, pink, purple, blue

Shelf life: 5-7 days
Season of growth: Summer

Easy to pair with ★★☆☆☆

Fragrancy ★☆☆☆☆

Thorny ★☆☆☆☆

Durability ★★★☆☆

Pairs well with: dahlias, roses,
ranunculus, Italian ruscus, eucalyptus

AMARANTHIS (HANGING)

pronounced a·muh·ran·thuhs

Colors: White, green, burgundy, bronze

Shelf life: 5-7 days
Season of growth: Summer-fall

Easy to pair with ★★☆☆☆

Fragrancy ★☆☆☆☆

Thorny ★☆☆☆☆

Durability ★★★☆☆

Pairs well with: protea, roses,
ranunculus, Italian ruscus, monstera

AMARANTHUS (UPRIGHT)

pronounced a·muh·ran·thuhs

Colors: Bronze, burgundy, green

Shelf life: 5-7 days
Season of growth: Summer-fall

Easy to pair with

Fragrancy

Thorny

Durability   ★★★☆☆

Pairs well with: protea, roses,
ranunculus, Italian ruscus, monstera

AMARYLLIS

pronounced a·mr·i·luhs

Colors: Red, white, pink, salmon, apricot, burgundy, multi color

Shelf life: 5-7 days
Season of growth: Winter-spring

Easy to pair with ★★☆☆☆

Fragrancy ★★☆☆☆

Thorny ★☆☆☆☆

Durability ★★★☆☆

Pairs well with: hydrangea, roses,
ranunculus, Italian ruscus, cedar

ANEMONE

pronounced uh·neh·muh·nee

Colors: White, magenta, purple, red, pink

Shelf life: 3-5 days
Season of growth: Summer-fall

Easy to pair with

Fragrancy

Thorny

Durability

Pairs well with: thistle, roses,
privet berries, Italian ruscus, eucalyptus

CALLA LILIES

pronounced ka·luh li·leez

Colors: White, pink, purple, orange, yellow, multi color

Shelf life: 3-5 days
Season of growth: Summer-fall

Easy to pair with	★★★☆☆
Fragrancy	★☆☆☆☆
Thorny	★☆☆☆☆
Durability	★★★☆☆

Pairs well with: hydrangea, roses,
stock, Italian ruscus, salal

COCKSCOMB

pronounced kaaks·kowm

Colors: White, yellow, orange, red, purple

Shelf life: 7-10 days
Season of growth: Fall

Easy to pair with ★★☆☆☆

Fragrancy ★☆☆☆☆

Thorny ★☆☆☆☆

Durability ★★★☆☆

Pairs well with: protea, roses,
amaranths, Italian ruscus, monstera

DAHLIA

pronounced da·lee·uh

Colors: Peach, red, lavender, white, yellow, orange, pink, multi color

Shelf life: 3-5 days
Season of growth: Fall

Easy to pair with ★★★☆☆

Fragrancy ★★☆☆☆

Thorny ★☆☆☆☆

Durability ★☆☆☆☆

Pairs well with: Stock, roses,
ranunculus, Italian ruscus, eucalyptus

FOX GLOVE

pronounced faaks·gluhv

Colors: Red, pink, yellow, white, purple

Shelf life: 3-5 days
Season of growth: Summer

Easy to pair with	★★★☆☆
Fragrancy	★★★☆☆
Thorny	★☆☆☆☆
Durability	★★★☆☆

Pairs well with: Dahlias, roses,
ranunculus, Italian ruscus, eucalyptus

FREESIA

pronounced free·zhuh

Colors: White, cream, yellow, orange, red, pink, lavender, purple

Shelf life: 3-5 days
Season of growth: Spring-summer

Easy to pair with	★★★☆☆
Fragrancy	★★★★☆
Thorny	★☆☆☆☆
Durability	★★☆☆☆

Pairs well with: Dahlias, roses,
hydrangea, Italian ruscus, eucalyptus

HELLEBORE

pronounced heh·luh·bor

Colors: White, green, pink, apricot, and purple, multi color

Shelf life: 3-5 days
Season of growth: Winter-spring

Easy to pair with ★★★☆☆

Fragrancy ★★★☆☆

Thorny ★☆☆☆☆

Durability ★★☆☆☆

Pairs well with: Dahlias, roses,
ranunculus, Italian ruscus, eucalyptus

JASMINE

pronounced jaz·muhn

Colors: White, pink, yellow

Shelf life: 3-5 days
Season of growth: Summer

Easy to pair with	★★☆☆☆
Fragrancy	★★★★☆
Thorny	★☆☆☆☆
Durability	★★☆☆☆

Pairs well with: Dahlias, roses,
ranunculus, Italian ruscus, eucalyptus

LEUCADENDRON "CONE FLOWER"

pronounced loo·kuh·den·druhn

Colors: Red, yellow

Shelf life: 5-7 days
Season of growth: Spring-summer

Easy to pair with

Fragrancy

Thorny

Durability

Pairs well with: Protea, roses,
ranunculus, Italian ruscus, monstera

LISIANTHUS

pronounced li·see·an·thuhs

Colors: Pink, purple and white, multi color

Shelf life: 3-5 days
Season of growth: Summer-fall

Easy to pair with

Fragrancy ★★★☆☆

Thorny ★☆☆☆☆

Durability

Pairs well with: Hydrangea, roses,
peonies, Italian ruscus, eucalyptus

MAGNOLIA FLOWER

pronounced mag·now·lee·uh

Colors: Dark green, brown

Shelf life: 7-10 days
Season of growth: Year round

Easy to pair with

Fragrancy

Thorny

Durability

Pairs well with: Roses, hydrangea, carnations

MARIGOLDS

pronounced meh·ruh·gowldz

Colors: Orange, yellow

Shelf life: 5-7 days
Season of growth: Summer-fall

Easy to pair with ★★☆☆☆

Fragrancy ★★★★☆

Thorny ★☆☆☆☆

Durability ★★★☆☆

Pairs well with: Stock, roses,
ranunculus, Italian ruscus, baker fern

MIMOSA

pronounced muh·mow·suh

Colors: Yellow, pink, purple

Shelf life: 3-5 days
Season of growth: Summer

Easy to pair with	★★★☆☆
Fragrancy	★☆☆☆☆
Thorny	★☆☆☆☆
Durability	★★☆☆☆

Pairs well with: Tulips, roses,
ranunculus, salal, eucalyptus

ORNITHOGALUM

pronounced or·nuh·thuh·ga·luhm

Colors: White, yellow, orange

Shelf life: 3-5 days
Season of growth: Spring-summer

Easy to pair with	★★★☆☆
Fragrancy	★☆☆☆☆
Thorny	★☆☆☆☆
Durability	★★☆☆☆

Pairs well with: Roses, hydrangea,
carnation, Italian ruscus, eucalyptus

POPPY

pronounced paa·pee

Colors: Red, orange, yellow, pink, purple

Shelf life: 3-5 days
Season of growth: Summer-fall

Easy to pair with	★★★☆☆
Fragrancy	★☆☆☆☆
Thorny	★☆☆☆☆
Durability	★★☆☆☆

Pairs well with: Roses, solidago,
ranunculus, Italian ruscus, eucalyptus

RANUNCULUS

pronounced ruh·nuhng·kyuh·luhs

Colors: White, yellow, apricot, pink, orange, red, burgundy

Shelf life: 3-5 days
Season of growth: Summer-fall

Easy to pair with ★★★★☆

Fragrancy ★★☆☆☆

Thorny ★☆☆☆☆

Durability ★★★☆☆

Pairs well with: Anemones, roses,
peonies, Italian ruscus, eucalyptus

SCABIOSA

pronounced ska·bee·ow·suh

Colors: Red, purple, lavender, pink, white

Shelf life: 3-5 days
Season of growth: Spring-summer

Easy to pair with  ★★☆☆☆

Fragrancy ★☆☆☆☆

Thorny ★☆☆☆☆

Durability  ★★☆☆☆

Pairs well with: Sweet pea, roses, thistle,
Italian ruscus, eucalyptus

STOCK

pronounced staak

Colors: White, cream, peach, fuchsia, pink, lavender, purple, multi color

Shelf life: 3-5 days
Season of growth: Spring-summer

Easy to pair with ★★★☆☆

Fragrancy ★★★★☆

Thorny ★☆☆☆☆

Durability ★★☆☆☆

Pairs well with: Sweet pea, roses,
ranunculus, Italian ruscus, eucalyptus

STEPHANOTIS

pronounced steh·fuh·now·tuhs

Colors: White

Shelf life: 3-5 days
Season of growth: Spring-summer

Easy to pair with ★★☆☆☆

Fragrancy ★★☆☆☆

Thorny ★☆☆☆☆

Durability ★★☆☆☆

Pairs well with: Roses, hydrangea,
carnations, Italian ruscus, eucalyptus

SWEET PEA

pronounced sweet·pee

Colors: Red, pink, blue, white, lavender

Shelf life: 3-5 ays
Season of growth: Year round

Easy to pair with ★★★☆☆

Fragrancy ★★★☆☆

Thorny ★☆☆☆☆

Durability ★★☆☆☆

Pairs well with: Peonies, roses,
carnations, Italian ruscus, eucalyptus

Tropical Flowers

ANTHURIUM

pronounced an·thear·ee·uhm

Colors: Pink, orange, red, green, purple, black, yellow
salmon, brown, blue, multi color

Shelf life: 7-10 days

Season of growth: Summer-fall

Easy to pair with ★★★☆☆

Fragrancy ★☆☆☆☆

Thorny ★☆☆☆☆

Durability ★★★★★

Pairs well with: Orchids, roses,
ranunculus, Italian ruscus, aspidistra

BEEHIVE GINGER

pronounced bee·hive jin·jr

One color: Brown, yellow, orange, red, pink, multi

Shelf life: 10-14 days
Season of growth: Spring- fall

Easy to pair with ★★☆☆☆

Fragrancy ★☆☆☆☆

Thorny ★☆☆☆☆

Durability ★★★★☆

Pairs well with: Protea, roses,
orchids, Italian ruscus, monstera

BIRDS OF PARADISE

pronounced burdz uhv peh·ruh·dise

One color: Blue, orange, red, purple

Shelf life: 5-7 days
Season of growth: Winter-summer

Easy to pair with	★★☆☆☆
Fragrancy	★☆☆☆☆
Thorny	★☆☆☆☆
Durability	★★★☆☆

Pairs well with: Protea, roses,
ginger, Italian ruscus, monstera

GINGER

pronounced jin·jr

Colors: Red, orange, yellow, pink

Shelf life: 5-7 days
Season of growth: Summer

Easy to pair with   ★★★☆☆

Fragrancy   ★★★★☆

Thorny   ★☆☆☆☆

Durability   ★★★★★

Pairs well with: Protea, roses,
birds of paradise, Italian ruscus, monstera

GREVILLEA

pronounced gruh·vi·lee·uh

Colors: White, pink, yellow, orange

Shelf life: 5-7 days
Season of growth: Summer

Easy to pair with   ★★☆☆☆

Fragrancy   ★☆☆☆☆

Thorny   ★☆☆☆☆

Durability   ★★★★☆

Pairs well with: Protea, anthurium,
birds of paradise, Italian ruscus, monstera

HELICONIA

pronounced heh·luh·kow·nee·uh

Colors: White, blue, magenta, purple, green, pink

Shelf life: 3-5 days
Season of growth: Winter-fall

Easy to pair with	★★☆☆☆
Fragrancy	★☆☆☆☆
Thorny	★☆☆☆☆
Durability	★★★☆☆

Pairs well with: Protea, roses,
orchids, Italian ruscus, monstera

Cymbidium

Dendrobium

Phalaenopsis

ORCHID

pronounced or·kuhd

Colors: Purple, lavender, pink, red, white, orange, yellow, green, brown, multi

Shelf life: 3-5 days
Season of growth: Spring-summer

Easy to pair with ★★☆☆☆

Fragrancy ★★☆☆☆

Thorny ★☆☆☆☆

Durability ★★☆☆☆

Pairs well with: Protea, roses,
hydrangea, aspidistra, monstera

King   Pincushions

PROTEA

pronounced prow·tee·uh

Colors: Pink, red, white, cream, yellow

Shelf life: 5-7 days
Season of growth: Fall-spring

Easy to pair with

Fragrancy

Thorny

Durability

Pairs well with: Orchids, roses,
ginger, Italian ruscus, monstera

Garden Flowers

ASTILBE

pronounced uh·stil·bee

Colors: White, pink, peach, red, purple

Shelf life: 3-5 days
Season of growth: Summer-fall

Easy to pair with

Fragrancy

Thorny

Durability

Pairs well with: Peonies, roses,
ranunculus, Italian ruscus, eucalyptus

AGAPANTHUS

pronounced a·guh·pan·thuhs

Colors: Blue, purple, white

Shelf life: 3-5 days
Season of growth: Summer-fall

Easy to pair with ★★☆☆☆

Fragrancy ★★☆☆☆

Thorny ★☆☆☆☆

Durability ★★☆☆☆

Pairs well with: Delphinium, hydrangea,
Italian ruscus, eucalyptus

AZALEA

pronounced uh·zay·lee·uh

Colors: White, purple, pink, red, orange, yellow

Shelf life: 5-7 days
Season of growth: Spring

Easy to pair with ★★★☆☆

Fragrancy ★★★★☆

Thorny ★☆☆☆☆

Durability ★★☆☆☆

Pairs well with: Hyacinth, daffodils

BLACK EYED SUSAN

pronounced blak ide soo·zn

Colors: Red, orange, yellow

Shelf life: 5-7 days
Season of growth: Summer-fall

Easy to pair with ★★★☆☆

Fragrancy ★☆☆☆☆

Thorny ★☆☆☆☆

Durability ★★★☆☆

Pairs well with: Sunflower, zinnia,
salal, Italian ruscus

BUPLEURUM

pronounced boo·plur·uhm

Colors: Green

Shelf life: 3-5 days
Season of growth: Summer

Easy to pair with

Fragrancy

Thorny

Durability

Pairs well with: Sunflowers, roses,
gerbera daisies, Italian ruscus, eucalyptus

CHAMOMILE

pronounced ka·muh·mile

One color: White and yellow center

Shelf life: 3-5 days
Season of growth: Summer-fall

Easy to pair with

Fragrancy

Thorny

Durability

Pairs well with: Gerbera daisies, sunflowers,
ranunculus, salal, eucalyptus

CLEMATIS

pronounced kleh·muh·tuhs

One color: Purple, blue, pink, white, red, multicolor

Shelf life: 3-5 days
Season of growth: Summer-fall

Easy to pair with	★★★☆☆
Fragrancy	★★★☆☆
Thorny	★☆☆☆☆
Durability	★★☆☆☆

Pairs well with: Roses, hydrangea,
ranunculus, salal, eucalyptus

DAFFODILS

pronounced da·fuh·dilz

Colors: White, pink and orange, yellow, multi

Shelf life: 3-5 days
Season of growth: Spring

Easy to pair with	★★★☆☆
Fragrancy	★★☆☆☆
Thorny	★☆☆☆☆
Durability	★★☆☆☆

Pairs well with: Hydrangea, roses,
solidago, israeli ruscus, salal

ECHINACEA

pronounced eh·kuh·nay·shuh

Colors: Purple, pink, salmon, orange, yellow, white, multi

Shelf life: 3-5 days
Season of growth: Summer-fall

Easy to pair with ★★★☆☆

Fragrancy ★★☆☆☆

Thorny ★☆☆☆☆

Durability ★★☆☆☆

Pairs well with: Zinnias, delphinium,
solidago, Italian ruscus, salal

FORGET ME NOTS "SCORPION GRASS"

pronounced fr·get mee naats

Colors: Blue, white, pink, yellow

Shelf life: 3-5 days
Season of growth: Spring

Easy to pair with ★★★☆☆

Fragrancy ★★☆☆☆

Thorny ★☆☆☆☆

Durability ★★☆☆☆

Pairs well with: Hydrangea, roses

GARDENIAS

pronounced gaar·dee·nyuh

Colors: White, red, pink, light yellow

Shelf life: 5-7 days
Season of growth: Summer

Easy to pair with	★★★★★
Fragrancy	★★★★★
Thorny	★★★★★
Durability	★★★★★

Pairs well with: Orchids, roses, hydrangea,
italian ruscus, eucalyptus

GOMPHRENA

pronounced gaam·free·nuh

Colors: Red, pink, purple, light purple, white .

Shelf life: 7-10 days
Season of growth: Summer-fall

Easy to pair with   ★★★☆☆

Fragrancy   ★☆☆☆☆

Thorny   ★☆☆☆☆

Durability   ★★★★☆

Pairs well with: Amaranths, tulip, zinnia,
Italian ruscus, eucalyptus

HEATHER

pronounced heh·thr

Colors: White, purple, pink

Shelf life: 5-7 days
Season of growth: Summer

Easy to pair with ★★☆☆☆

Fragrancy ★★☆☆☆

Thorny ★☆☆☆☆

Durability ★★☆☆☆

Pairs well with: Peonies, carnations, roses

HIBISCUS

pronounced hai·bi·skuhs

Colors: orange, yellow, red, pink and multicolor

Shelf life: 5-7 days
Season of growth: Spring-summer

Easy to pair with ★★☆☆☆

Fragrancy ★★★★☆

Thorny ★☆☆☆☆

Durability ★★☆☆☆

Pairs well with: Lilies, peonies, allium

HYACINTH

pronounced hai·uh·snth

Colors: White, cream, pink, rose, apricot, lavender, blue, purple, burgundy

Shelf life: 5-7 days
Season of growth: Spring

Easy to pair with ★★☆☆☆

Fragrancy ★★★★☆

Thorny ★☆☆☆☆

Durability ★★★☆☆

Pairs well with: Tulips, carnations,
cala lilies, Italian ruscus, eucalyptus

KALANCHOE

pronounced ka·luhn·kow·ee

Colors: Red, orange, yellow, green, white, pink, lilac, salmon, multi color

Shelf life: 20-30 days
Season of growth: Spring

Easy to pair with	★★☆☆☆
Fragrancy	★★☆☆☆
Thorny	★☆☆☆☆
Durability	★★★☆☆

Pairs well with: Hyacinth, daffodills

KALE

pronounced kayl

Colors: Dark green, light green, purple

Shelf life: 20-30 days
Season of growth: Spring-fall

Easy to pair with ★★☆☆☆

Fragrancy ★☆☆☆☆

Thorny ★☆☆☆☆

Durability ★★★☆☆

Pairs well with: Hyacinth, daffodills

LAMBS EAR

pronounced lams err

Colors: Silver/grey

Shelf life: 3-5 days
Season of growth: Spring-fall

Easy to pair with

Fragrancy

Thorny

Durability

Pairs well with: Pansys, daffodills

KANGAROO PAW

pronounced kang·gr·oo paa

Colors: Yellow, orange, red, pink, purple

Shelf life: 5-7 days
Season of growth: Spring-fall

Easy to pair with

Fragrancy

Thorny

Durability

LAVENDER

pronounced la·vuhn·dr

Colors: Light purple

Shelf life: 3-5 days
Season of growth: Summer-fall

Easy to pair with ★★★☆☆

Fragrancy ★★★★★

Thorny ★☆☆☆☆

Durability ★★☆☆☆

Pairs well with: Sunflowers, zinnias,
thistle, Italian ruscus, eucalyptus

LILAC

pronounced lai·lak

Colors: Light purple, magenta, pink, white

Shelf life: 3-5 days
Season of growth: Spring-summer

Easy to pair with   ★★★☆☆

Fragrancy   ★★★★☆

Thorny   ★☆☆☆☆

Durability   ★★☆☆☆

Pairs well with: Ranunculus, roses,
carnations, Italian ruscus, monstera

LOTUS

pronounced low·tuhs

Colors: white, pink, yellow, red, blue, purple, multi

Bloom time: 2-5 months
Season of growth: Summer-fall

Easy to pair with ★★★☆☆

Fragrancy ★★★★☆

Thorny ★☆☆☆☆

Durability ★★☆☆☆

Pairs well with: Chrysanthemums, lambs ear

LILY OF THE VALLEY (CONVALLARIA MAJALIS)

pronounced li·lee uhv thu val·ee

Colors: Blue, purple, white, pink.

Shelf life: 3-5 days
Season of growth: Spring

Easy to pair with ★☆☆☆☆

Fragrancy ★★★☆☆

Thorny ★☆☆☆☆

Durability ★★☆☆☆

Pairs well with: Ranunculus, roses,
carnations, Italian ruscus, eucalyptus

PANSEY

pronounced pan·zee

Colors: Yellow, red, blue, purple, pink, orange, white

Shelf life: 3-8 months
Season of growth: Spring-summer

Easy to pair with ★★★☆☆

Fragrancy ★★☆☆☆

Thorny ★☆☆☆☆

Durability ★★★☆☆

Pairs well with: Chrysanthemums, lambs ear

PHLOX PANICULATA

pronounced flaaks puh·ni·kyuh·laa·tuh

Colors: Pink, red, lavender, purple, orange, white

Shelf life: 3-8 months
Season of growth: Summer

Easy to pair with	★★★☆☆
Fragrancy	★★☆☆☆
Thorny	★☆☆☆☆
Durability	★★☆☆☆

Pairs well with: Roses, lisanthius, carnation

WISTERIA

pronounced wuh·stee·ree·uh

Colors: Purple, white, pink, blue

Shelf life: 3-5 days
Season of growth: Spring-summer

Easy to pair with ★☆☆☆☆

Fragrancy ★★☆☆☆

Thorny ★☆☆☆☆

Durability ★☆☆☆☆

VIOLET

pronounced vai·uh·luhts

Colors: blue, purple, pink, white, red, coral

Shelf life: 7-10 days
Season of growth: Winter-summer

Easy to pair with ★☆☆☆☆

Fragrancy ★★☆☆☆

Thorny ★☆☆☆☆

Durability ★☆☆☆☆

Pairs well with: Kalanchoe, daffodills

Dried Flowers

BUNNY TAIL

pronounced buh·nee tayl

Colors: White, blue, magenta, purple, green, pink

Shelf life: 5-7 days live, 1 year dried
Season of growth: Spring-summer

Easy to pair with ★★★☆☆

Frangrency ★☆☆☆☆

Thorny ★☆☆☆☆

Durability ★★★★★

Pairs well with: Protea, roses,
ranunculus, Italian ruscus, monstera

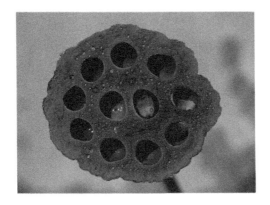

LOTUS POD

pronounced low·tuhs pod

Colors; Brown

Shelf life: 7-10 days live, 3 years dried

Season of growth: Summer

Easy to pair with   ★ ★ ☆ ☆ ☆

Fragrancy   ★ ☆ ☆ ☆ ☆

Thorny   ★ ☆ ☆ ☆ ☆

Durability   ★ ★ ★ ★ ★

Pairs well with: Gypsophila, hydrangea, roses, dried palm leaf, pampas grass

PAMPAS GRASS

pronounced pam·puhs gras

Colors; Yellow, pink, silver, peach, cream

Shelf life: 7-10 days live, 3 years dried

Season of growth: Summer-fall

Easy to pair with	★★★☆☆
Fragrancy	★☆☆☆☆
Thorny	★☆☆☆☆
Durability	★★★★★

Pairs well with: Gypsophila, hydrangea, roses, bunny tail, Italian ruscus

PALM LEAF

pronounced paam leef

Colors; Cream

Shelf life: 7-10 days live, 3 years dried

Season of growth: Summer-fall

Easy to pair with ★★★☆☆

Fragrancy ★☆☆☆☆

Thorny ★☆☆☆☆

Durability ★★★☆☆

Pairs well with: Gypsophila, hydrangea,
roses, bunny tail, pampas grass

Greenery

ARALIA

pronounced uh·ray·lee·uh

Colors: Dark green

Shelf life: 7-10 days
Season of growth: Summer

Easy to pair with

Fragrancy

Thorny

Durability

Pairs well with: Protea, orchids, birds of paradise

ARECA PALM

pronounced uh·ree·kuh paam

Colors: Dark green

Shelf life: 7-10 days
Season of growth: Summer

Easy to pair with	
Fragrancy	
Thorny	
Durability	

Pairs well with: Protea, orchids, birds of paradise

ASPARAGUS "MING" FERN

pronounced uh·speh·ruh·guhs furn

Colors: Dark green

Shelf life: 7-10 days
Season of growth: Summer-fall

Easy to pair with	★★☆☆☆
Fragrancy	★☆☆☆☆
Thorny	★★★☆☆
Durability	★★☆☆☆

Pairs well with: Hydrangea, sunflowers, roses

BAKER FERN

pronounced bay·kr furn

Colors: Dark green

Shelf life: 7-10 days
Season of growth: Year round

Easy to pair with

Frangrency

Thorny

Durability

Pairs well with: Hydrangea, sunflowers, daisies

BOXWOOD

pronounced baaks·wud

Colors: Dark green

Shelf life: 7-10 days
Season of growth: Year round

Easy to pair with

Fragrancy

Thorny

Durability

Pairs well with: Roses, Hydrangea, tulips

CEDAR

pronounced see·dr

Colors: Green

Shelf life: 7-10 days
Season of growth: Winter

Easy to pair with

Fragrancy

Thorny

Durability

Pairs well with: Tulips, roses, hydrangea

DUSTY MILLER

pronounced duh·stee mi·lr

Colors: Silver/gray

Shelf life: 1-2 days
Season of growth: Summer

Easy to pair with

Fragrancy

Thorny

Durability

Pairs well with: Anemone, roses, thistle, hydrangea

EMERALD

pronounced eh·mr·uhld

Colors: Dark green

Shelf life: 7-10 days
Season of growth: Summer

Easy to pair with

Fragrancy

Thorny

Durability

Pairs well with: Gladiolus, hydrangea, roses

Parviolia

Silver Dollar

Seeded

Baby Blue

Feather Willow

Gunni

EUCALYPTUS

pronounced u·kuh·lip·tuhs

Colors: Blue/silver

Shelf life: 3-5 days
Season of growth: Summer-fall

Easy to pair with ★★★☆☆

Fragrancy ★★★★☆

Thorny ★☆☆☆☆

Durability ★★☆☆☆

Pairs well with: Ranunculus, roses, hydrangea

FOXTAIL MILLET

pronounced faak·stayl mi·luht

Colors: Light green, tan

Shelf life: 7-10 days
Season of growth: Summer-fall

Easy to pair with   ★★★☆☆

Fragrancy   ★☆☆☆☆

Thorny   ★☆☆☆☆

Durability   ★★★★☆

Pairs well with: Zinnias, hydrangea, sunflowers

HUCKLEBERRY

pronounced huh·kuhl·beh·ree

Colors: Dark green

Shelf life: 7-10 days
Season of growth: Winter-spring

Easy to pair with ★★★☆☆

Fragrancy ★☆☆☆☆

Thorny ★☆☆☆☆

Durability ★★★★☆

Pairs well with: Roses, hydrangea, Sunflowers

IRISH MILLET

pronounced ai·ruhsh mi·luht

Colors: Light green, tan

Shelf life: 7-10 days
Season of growth: Summer-fall

Easy to pair with ★★★☆☆

Fragrancy ★☆☆☆☆

Thorny ★☆☆☆☆

Durability ★★★★☆

Pairs well with: Roses, hydrangea, sunflowers

IVY

pronounced ai·vee

Colors: Dark green, light green

Shelf life: 7-10 days
Season of growth: Summer-fall

Easy to pair with	★★★☆☆
Fragrancy	★☆☆☆☆
Thorny	★☆☆☆☆
Durability	★★★★☆

Pairs well with: Roses, hydrangea, sunflowers

JUNIPER

pronounced joo·nuh·pr

Colors: Dark green

Shelf life: 7-10 days
Season of growth: Winter

Easy to pair with

Fragrancy

Thorny

Durability

Pairs well with: Roses, hydrangea, cedar

MAIDEN HAIR FERN

pronounced may·dn hehr furn

Colors: Green

Shelf life: 3-5 days
Season of growth: Year round

Easy to pair with

Fragrancy

Thorny

Durability

Pairs well with: Roses, hydrangea, carnations

MONSTERA

pronounced maan·str·uh

Colors: Dark green

Shelf life: 7-10 days
Season of growth: Summer

Easy to pair with	★★★☆☆
Fragrancy	★☆☆☆☆
Thorny	★☆☆☆☆
Durability	★★★★☆

Pairs well with: Protea, birds of paradise, ginger

MYRTLE

pronounced mur·tl

Colors: Dark green/burgundy

Shelf life: 7-10 days
Season of growth: Spring-summer

Easy to pair with

Fragrancy

Thorny

Durability

Pairs well with: Protea, orchids, cala lilies

PINE

pronounced pine

Colors: Dark green

Shelf life: 5-7 days
Season of growth: Year round

Easy to pair with ★★★☆☆

Fragrancy ★★★★☆

Thorny ★★★☆☆

Durability ★★★☆☆

Pairs well with: Thistle, hydrangea, roses, cedar

PODOCARPUS

pronounced paa·duh·kaar·puh

Colors: Dark green

Shelf life: 5-7 days
Season of growth: Spring-fall

Easy to pair with	★★★☆☆
Fragrancy	★★☆☆☆
Thorny	★★☆☆☆
Durability	★★★☆☆

Pairs well with: Tulips, roses, salal

Italian   Israeli

RUSCUS

pronounced ruh·skuhs

Colors: Dark green

Shelf life: 3-5 days
Season of growth: Year round

Easy to pair with ★★★★☆

Fragrancy ★☆☆☆☆

Thorny ★☆☆☆☆

Durability ★★★☆☆

Pairs well with: Ranunculus, roses, carnations

SALAL (LEMON LEAF)

pronounced suh·laal

Colors: Green

Shelf life: 5-7 days
Season of growth: Summer

Easy to pair with

Fragrancy

Thorny

Durability

Pairs well with: Protea, birds of paradise, ginger

SPRENGERI "ASPARAGUS FERN"

pronounced spr·ing·er·ai

Colors: Dark green

Shelf life: 5-7 days
Season of growth: Summer-fall

Easy to pair with   ★★★☆☆

Fragrancy   ★☆☆☆☆

Thorny   ★★★★☆

Durability   ★★☆☆☆

Pairs well with: Thistle, sunflowers, roses

SWORD FERN

pronounced sord furn

Colors: Green

Shelf life: 5-7 days
Season of growth: Spring-fall

Easy to pair with

Fragrancy

Thorny

Durability

Pairs well with: Anthurium, sunflowers, roses

WHITE PINE

pronounced wite pine

Colors: Dark green

Shelf life: 5-7 days
Season of growth: Year round

Easy to pair with	★★★☆☆
Fragrancy	★★★★☆
Thorny	★★★☆☆
Durability	★★★☆☆

Pairs well with: Thistle, hydrangea, roses, cedar

Thank you

for using my guide!

For more flower tips and florist business advice,
check out my *YouTube channel @aleexischristine*
and follow me on *Instagram @flowersbyalexis*

About the Author

Alexis Christine is the author behind *Flower Identification*. She is a florist, YouTuber, engineer, writer, and artist. Her work can be seen across multiple social media platforms where she shares her floral design experience and gives florist tips and advice to beginner florists and experienced designers. Alexis has been a florist since 2014. She started out as a design assistant in a busy flower shop in a suburb of Philadelphia. You can visit her online at *www.flowersbyalexisfba.com, Instagram @flowersbyalexis, and on her YouTube Channel, @aleexischristine*

harpercolins.com

Made in the USA
Las Vegas, NV
01 April 2024

88120160R00085